Credo

and Other Poems

Francis Patrick Sullivan

Sheed & Ward

Kansas City

Sheed & Ward™ is a service of The National Catholic Reporter Publishing Company.

━━━━━━━━━━━━━━━━━━◆━━━━━━━━━━━━━━━━━━

Library of Congress Cataloguing-in-Publication Data

Sullivan, Francis, 1929-
    Credo, and other poems / Francis Patrick Sullivan.
       p.   cm.
    ISBN: 1-55612-805-3 (pbk. : alk. paper)
    1. Christian poetry, American.   I. Title.
   PS3569.U347C74   1995
   811'.54—dc20   95-35925
                                                      CIP

━━━━━━━━━━━━━━━━━━◆━━━━━━━━━━━━━━━━━━

Published by: Sheed & Ward
                  115 E. Armour Blvd.
                  P.O. Box 419492
                  Kansas City, MO 64141-6492

To order, call: (800) 333-7373

Cover design and interior art by Aileen Callahan.

Contents

People

Place

Relation

Stations of the Cross
Drawings by Aileen Callahan

Credo

Words. In a tropical tank,
they are the lyrefish;
in a hailstorm,
they are the hit sounds on metal;
in me, they are the whiskers
on a catfish,
they are the tongue of a snake,
or feelers,
as on crabs or butterflies,
or they are probes,
person to person, for nourishment,
or pups at tits or tiny forks
at claw meat,
or they are raw fingers from
tombstone rubbing,
or splitting rocks for fern prints,
or shucking lies.

Graces

Irish Ancestry

My people on one side were silent.
I stood later in their hills
and watched the sea work the strand,
the bitter sea for them.
They told it nothing of what they felt,
nor the orchards, nor the roses,
nor the drip of the quick rain.
They told sex nothing of the flush
on their cheeks, of their own pregnancies
alongside nanny goats and ewes.
That was the silence I received.
To this day it will not speak.
There is school speaking in me now,
there are rules, there is the flavor
of fields worked by other bees,
a savagery controlled by a rhythm,
but ready to sting once and die.
I can last in their silence.
Words are more like rain, they knew,
words broke on things,
the voice that said them broke.

Pushing Sixty

I want the next moment,
not the last one,
a shooting star, not a bench mark,
something is not yet said,
maybe a scream,
maybe an indictment,
maybe the "geez" of astronauts
at the bareness of space,
the weightlessness they have become.
The last word
is not the birch outside the house
leeched by its own seeds
a week in May.
It is after, in October,
the birch with peeled bark, hard resin,
bare branches, when a bird on one
strops its beak from a gnat,
the split second.

News of More Terror

It's a day to be with a dog,
maybe smell things also in the air,
live on one sensation.
The apples are still bitter,
the berries have a slight rot,
some of the leaves are souring.
A woman has been by here,
she uses sachet, not perfume,
and someone has been lying,
a paper says so, in a trash barrel.
The dog has lost me,
he crashes back out of a hedge
and finds me halted. I am smelling death
down to the level of dog.
Below him there is life,
to yellow fungus in the crotches of trees.
Above him there is degradation.
I bend to tie my shoe,
let the dog lick my face
into a new shape.

Comes the Catch

I see a light purple.
The sun is gone.
The winter sky contracts
into a chill.
I have to move,
not watch it go black.

I knew someone in Rome,
an old priest
who sat with the sun late
every winter day,
right down to an inch
above the seventh hill
to the west of the city.
Then he left the roof
to keep that margin.

But I stayed
to watch it sink,
a circular saw
swallowed live by a log,
then bang, the evening star,
hung there like a gull
over scraps.

I Ching

I do not find myself, not anymore,
in twisted cypress trees spotted with red fungus,
their roots down through rocks to the suckings of surf
and dead man's float of seaweed;

and not in the hang of my scrotum;
and not in the biting of my tongue;
and not in the way I call the dog.

I am now like an effect, a lap harp,
a screech of tires; the images have turned on me.

I am someone's cross, the hawk spread,
hung on wire to scare, and bitterly deceived;
someone's skid marks knotted into arabic script;
someone's brain breaking as he pats a flowering tree.

I am a part of speech for quartz and pulp and snail.

But back of me, a door, open, out into space.

Elegy. My Father's Ocean.

He is dead. I am fierce to feed through my skin,
delicious water, sand, light.
There are years left of tides' thick and thin flesh
on skeleton sand underneath before I am dead too,
and make someone else fierce to eat carnality
before they are eaten by it.
But I am fasting. Because he loved the salt water
I spit out, not from nausea, but fear of choking on it.
I swim and spit along a sandbar near a fog line,
no one else, seawards, then I run back
heeling the fat sandbar. The fog is black a mile off.
I am not what he is, nor this is.
I am a sound no one makes with a full mouth.
Teeth and tongue must be clear, throat clear, lungs,
the skin tight and chill, but the belly warm and safe
from shivers. My sound is not gull, not teel, not buoy.
It is you! you! with pauses, with utter certitude
someone will fill them, now or never.

Venice. Scuola di San Rocco.

The painting was a Tintoretto,
marked Magdalen, but I saw a Rembrandt,
the Suicide of Lucretia,
a look-alike, pointing a dagger at herself,
not a bible, by a stream in a woods.
I fooled myself in the low light,
walked through the whole gallery fooled,
fifty two biblical subjects,
but nervous about the one who was not.
She was Magdalen when I checked.
But I still saw Lucretia.
Magdalen fasted to the brink for repair.
Lucretia crossed it.
There was no repair anyone could make her.
She is someplace not biblical.
No one will ever touch her again.
I once had my soul kill itself on me.
I held it to a creed.
It is in a place now out of reach.
But is present,
like the cat that licks its paws
on the hood of a car.
What's left of me is fit for life.
Everything can be repaired.

Except violation.
It is like an eternal fact,
the cat who moves out of reach,
who turns and looks and sees
I am not here.

After News of Cancer

Pick a few chestnuts, polish them for skin;
pinch some thistle seed for a head of hair,
some acorns for nipples, toadstools for hips,
you've seen the like in vegetable paintings.
Because a she can give you none of hers,
nor a he of his. So scavenge likenesses.
But afterwards, sit on a puddingstone rock
and think, think if a he or she is not
the master of their skin, why give death away?
Why not keep it like the salamander on your hand
which you turn and twist so the salamander
who wants up is always up! Until you stop
and it paws the air, sits a time deciding,
then jumps somewhere, and your hand is gone!

Anniversary Shot

I want the photo that shows the scar.
It is an innocent scar.
A cancer was cut out above my lip,
a neat, up and down slice.
It says nothing about war,
nothing about accident.
It speaks of seasons only,
of fruition or the rot to come.
I welcome it now,
though it may mean torture later,
the kind a man called ridiculous
and would not let us see him die.
My skin has closed well.
And this is the season for picking,
fruit for the table, not the compost heap,
and not for my own table either.
I have life from the death side.
It is in this scar on my face.
Delicious life, hung within reach.
Cut in, not cut out.

Cold Comfort. Irish.

The hoarser,
the better the message – sorry,
he was good,
it was a grace he died –
my strep-throat sound is
at home:

this is Fall,
this is a burial ground,
it is rife with colored leaves
and rusted hedges.

The words get through my throat,
not a kiss, but discreet, averted words,
to keep to myself what harms me,
not what counsels the widow to forget
the brute in pain
for the grace that stopped it.

I am not satisfied with grace,
someone with a horse pistol,
an animal with rolling eyes,
a calm maturity,
a flat sound lurching riderless

around a barn, then mercy,
a footprint filling with water,
lungs with the smell of gun.
But maybe I understand.
A second shot hits nothing.

Rome. To St. Mary Major's

There are few trees
along the tufa block streets.
Many birds dung them
and the sidewalks below,
making filthy circles.
But there are fountains
that lick themselves clean
with clear, clear water.
It comes from snow melt
along old aqueducts.
I scoop it from a trough
to make a puddle in which
to clean my shoe of dog.
I have a cold hand from it.
I have a cold heart
from being left out at night
like pots of cyclamen
that die in central heat.
The night air is filthy too,
but cold colors stay clear.
My shoe is now clean.
But my memory is not.
I scuff every rough surface,
every patch of sun.

Seasons

Choices

To move the rock,
I will have to bruise the lichen
which makes it look living,
green fuzz with orange spots
like the eyes of gila monsters.
But I want to add,
set this rock on new ones,
then thicken the flow of water near it
to spread the living green
with its orange eyes.
Maybe grow a fern.
But a fern would be too lush,
would lose me the arctic sense
of late August's bite.
It would arouse passion
for something not rock,
with teeth and tongue that do not
still things.

Zen Path. Hammondswood.

I.

Walk on dead leaves
in the trough. The thumbs of green
will be safe to each side,
and the leaves will be ground
to a noiseless gravel.
Later there will be geese-like green
knee high and flapping
as if you fed them on your visits.
So much else is selection for killing.
Or it just happens
as you look at names on trees
written on small tags,
minute purples and pinks squash
and stain your shoe.
It means a year's wait to see
if their forms escape and come back.
So many forms you know do not.
Though their names do.
But repeating names is futile,
not the same purple or pink
that stained you.

II.

I used to lift a twig
from the ground after new snow
to see the carbon trace of it.
The black lines were life,
the rotted leaves, the loam smell.
The snow was a mask.
But loam and leaves are masks now,
and life has no trace.
I see everything for the first time
and for the last.
I appear and disappear
to a thrilling beat or the beat
of a dead march on muffled drums.
This can go on.
There is no boredom to it.
There is fatigue, but a new sleep,
a new waking.
But there is also only watching.
If I move I frighten things,
they mask themselves,
and I am back to traces,
the careful lifting of what broke off
for what did not.

Autumn

Berries,
and weed flowers,
crows crouching on sidewalks
for worms,

my tongue is dry!

Lungs,
chafed and chafing cold air,
and seed shedding,
spin, plumb, float,

I have to leave!

Beads,
and tree bark,
and white of a branch stump,
and sawdust,

leave like you!

Soul State

I don't rake and bag leaves.
I let them pile up savage.
They want into the house,
small pieces of animal jaw
that won't let go my foot.
I hear them hit the window
at night, like a fish nose.
I wanted this state for a long time.
I didn't think it was feeble,
or snub like a revolver.
I thought it was string-taut,
hairless as pre-puberty.
There was a next it had to do
and wouldn't waste a motion.
Too much has fallen to burn.
Fire in leaves is too quiet.
The smoke is bitter not sweet.
The burner has to stay upwind
with a rake and keep feeding
the hiss, the smudge pot,
until the ashes are the question.
What next with ashes?
I can put my foot right in them,
never get bitten.

Destinies

Trees drop rubbish and turds.
People drop reddish leaves.
Anyway, the ground is littered
with the destinies of smell,
whatever my tricks of speech.
People and trees are lightened.
But I can't stay here long.
It's the people, not the trees.
There is no innocent log of them
left on some clean forest floor
where the fallen smell sweet.
Sweet for them is near the sea,
which cleans things out of sight.
I want to walk into it,
to know what it will do to me.
I want to walk out,
let water drip on the hard sand,
run its own way back.
I want its lesson in sense.
The ground is too slow, too brutal.
I have to turn my face.

A Lesson in Purpose

That dogwood holds its flesh
in May so long I despair.
Its blossom is old age doing its nails
while the car outside is honking.
Youth looks comic beside it,
like a basset hound
writhing in pleasure as one rubs it,
but doleful and wet in the chops.
That dogwood singles me out
and seats me and says: Look,
until the world is in your hand,
as it is in mine,
and nothing is under it,
then let your hand drop, but slowly.
See! Everything floats!

Love. Straight Talk Between Us.

Trees tell me be alone with the sources,
soil, wind, water, and whatever the light.
There is as much passion to it
as to single strand webs, hung across a trail,
to catch on the bridge of someone's nose,
and make them find it to pluck it off.
But tree is drastic. It latches on to no skin,
it catches on no mouth, it mixes with no spit,
though it has a raw nerve for every sense,
and there is absorption, even speech of a body kind,
and sex, but slowed to a ring a year.
I could walk the trails myself,
break the webs, do the spitting out,
but that's too late. Whoever made them is gone.

Rome. Bravado.

I bought cyclamen at a stall.
I need a cactus, green,
with knives for leaves, not lobes.
The seller may have one Monday.
She is young, thickened by her wool clothes
against the late winter. Meantime,
she bumps me towards a cactus
that has a hot red flower.
But I need something for later,
a sawtooth to tell me I have time left
to fiddle with contrasts.
I have a cousin who does not.
He is wasted from a cancer and all tubes,
but fiercely patient.
I left him and came here to teach
visions of afterlife,
as they were taught us by native peoples,
or left by them in color or stone.
I want the right cactus,
the cyclamen blooms only for a week,
then becomes stalks and leaves.
Love has not made a unity.
I am away when people die, or get so old
they forget their mothers.

If I get the right cactus to match
the plummeting cyclamen,
I can watch death and knives at work.
But a flower rise
right through their rattle.

Winter Mood

A tin can
inside a cyclone fence,
a bitter cold wind,
the scraping hop, skip, jump,
the silence,
the reverse clatter
on blacktop,
I cannot connect with them.
There are rusting leaves
under the teeth of the fence,
and jet engine racket over it
doubled by the cold
to thudding.
This is the truth.
A bus will come and take me,
its shock absorbers
pummeled and pummeling
the street,
but it will float me, shiver me,
drop me at an underground
where I can connect
with something that screeches
and hisses
like jaguars, like camels.

March

A house shouldn't leak,
we say, arranging buckets,
the ceiling will drop.
That slate the snow took with it
when the thaw came,
it's the hole maybe, or the drain
we didn't clean of leaves.
The house of worms leaks too.
The sidewalk is littered with them.
There are too few birds yet.
So there's no place to step
to look at the gutter and roof.
We can redo the plaster,
not the silk print wallpaper
nor the mahogany moulding.
Maybe we move to something simpler.
Or just watch the damage mount.

Talk

Psalm Sequence

I

My few words for you
are spun steel, that rough, that gray,
like a metal pot with a lid
and beads of sweat:
I cannot love you anymore on faith.
I know about those who do.
They are blind cure or kill,
like different mushrooms or herbs,
they never know which.
But there are loves greater
than my sweating pot
and its scratched steel.
I have heard yes and no be taps
on a drum no one can fake.
Or be wildflowers in thick grass
with poison oak and dragonflies –
stars, bells, pupils, tongues –
the purity of mulch.
Someone loves you from a heap.
You can smell it thicken you, dust,
fill your lungs and your head,
not with fever,
but with an odor that sticks.

II

You are not

the tit song in the maple,

not the lava

eating through orchards.

I am not.

But something clicks.

I love a living gray, like wings.

You love gestures.

Across space with hands,

or at table.

But we are large and small.

So I need time.

I love what I see,

the long throat,

the long hands flying or failing

and beached like ribs.

Your invitation is tragic,

but who else breathes

after the deaths,

shallow breaths at first,

then deep,

hands across your throat,

to tell me

wait, You will explain!

III

There is to be a trial,
not a jubilee;
I will do what I do until then,
live with other graces
and see if I am right against the law,
so the law is tried
and what escapes it proves me
to have been vital,
though said to have been lethal;
yet no time is left
after a trial; lives close;
a quick look back at events is all,
an effort to reclassify them;
the people are gone
who could change their minds;
and I am different;
I will never do again
what was lethal or vital;
the people are gone;
I forget the next thing.

IV

Maybe next
is rote, is no-choice life
or squeaky wheel or
bingo life,
or riotous, a wine pouch
and sweaty gaucho life,
or you, not these,
but you worked out by us
as lithographs,
or not worked out,
not stone,
cirrus and cool through pines
in fungoid light,
a silver-green shimmer,
or not, just skin life,
first to get, first to give,
around the eyes,
around the tongue,
or not, just stories,
with pauses where we recover
and drink,
but you do not,
you have to keep us
squirming.

V

You could tell the story
of someone who loved you
and turned it into a suicide,
which made you retch
and not say anything to him
when he came with his proof;
or of someone who hated you
and became a taxidermist,
of birds, the last of each kind,
to shame you in company;
or of someone like me
who puts words in your mouth,
or takes them out, soon after
someone else put them in,
just to get the ogre look
off your face so no one scares
who is good, and no one scoffs
who is bad, and the middle
group can offer you advice;
or of someone like you
who will let nothing settle
where it fell, but puts it back,
or out of reach, or under glass
where it glows, or in water
where it floats until the time
is perfect for it to let go.

VI

I panic

if I lose a horizon.

I can imagine looping

in a plane,

like a tick bird around a beast,

but not the loss of the hairline

between sea and sky.

So you cannot take me far,

though I want to go with you.

So I will practice.

But not alone.

Unless that's the essence,

no hairline,

just lack of limit.

But there has to be a you,

even dead silent.

If not,

there is the miracle

that I am you,

and I keep things apart

for my pleasure,

the few things I know,

the many I do not.

But the pain

is everywhere in everything

so my miracle is small.
I am not you.
At best, I am the dead silence
you provoke
when you are and are not
rabies or rapture
on that hairline fracture
in between,
where I do my walking.

People

Rogue Zen

A man stares for hours
at a white sheet of paper
to make the one stroke
with a brush and black ink.
Unable to, he rises,
goes to his vegetable board,
pares carrots, dices onions,
makes a pot of soup.
Meantime, a woman outside
leans against his wall
in the cold morning air,
her eyes closed, her head back,
the sun at her throat.

Fraticelli

It could never be a woman
who seduced them. It had to be Wisdom
who, when they were hard and biting
for her breasts, opened like a book not a sex
and showed the principles they bit for.
Wisdom they could see was a man
seated at a desk with a candle and skull
deciphering scripture.
They would never bite for that.
But in a window, someone combing her hair
or squatting near a wall for relief
or with a jug on her head,
her hands free, driving goats with a switch,
she was the whole law and prophets,
she was the cosmic piss.

Keats in Cairo (Notes)

There are goddess figurines
in gold and terra cotta
to guard King Tut's bust.
He is carved from wood
and painted luscious colors
to make of him a girl
the whole world can want.
But Nefertiti nearby, in stone,
with the sculptor's pen
still marking where to cut,
some want her more.
She is not yet finished.
His wood is cracked on top,
so his soul has left.
But she is still posing.
Her glass case is no defense.
There are kiss marks on it,
finger and forehead prints.
She is turning into flesh
brown as sugar in the raw.
She is as dead as he,
but her stone is hungry.

Teotihuacan: Where We Became Gods

I want some mineral water, with gas,
from dogged peddlers at my elbow,
not four-note flutes, not obsidian gods,
not silver bracelets for my wife,
I have no wife. My God is carnal enough.
I want some mineral water
so I can forget my mouth and the dust in it,
so I can keep looking at these ruins,
the pyramids, the squares, the crosses.
They too saw water make the difference clear
between the fixed and fugitive.
The whole place is a thirst that succeeds.
The wind rises at four every afternoon,
brings in rain to sweep the valley
the way a warrior would, slashing, salivating,
but it is the comedy, not tragedy of water,
it wriggles through mud like a snake.
And the corn stalks of the valley suck it in
like green lizards with fast tongues. Later,
people with fast teeth gnaw the flesh off the cob.
They keep their coffee-colored skin,
but underneath, have the golden glow of corn.
And they die as dried stalks do,
they must let the rain gouge the earth away,
but they rustle with defiance,
like their ruins.

Metro Station Exit: Mexico City

The roses are limp

in a heap on the sidewalk.

The man is limp

who squats and sells them.

The money is limp from hand to hand,

but in someone's fist

as he walks away

the roses are like rescued pups

with maybe a life ahead.

In the right vase.

The man had six left by dark.

He threw them in the trash.

Two street kids took them out,

washed them in a rain puddle

and sold them later

for a fraction.

I have them floating in a bowl.

A Theology

There is the sex of a form,
then there is not,
there is its sound beyond sex,
a hoot for company,
a listening,
as for safety cracks running
the ice of a lake,
then its hoot again
when the answers do not come,
then its dissolution,
the feathered lump and trail of ants,
the remorse of form
that the answers did not come,
then there is the stare
at who did not answer
but could have,
the space between anything and anything,
branches, rocks, fingers,
then the stare of space back,
stiffening into a test
of who blinks.

An American Dream

Someone sits on a rock
and cools her feet
in snow melt water in a creek bed.
It is not enough.
She orders the rock moved
and a basin made,
deep, and lined with sand
to control the mud
so she can stand up to her neck.
It is not enough.
The winter can come.
So she orders a glass dome
and heated air inside.
It is not enough.
So she orders a man in with her.
He is not enough.
A drought year dries the creek.
So she is bitter.
She believes in nothing,
even death, which she enters
with revenge in mind.

Wisdom

We wait out the weather inside, whatever it is.
Who wants even to breathe if it costs.
One man used to crack walnuts half the night during TV,
then wash the meat down with red wine.
There used to be left hard shapes in a black bowl,
a bed of fragments under them and echoes on top.
Something cracked him far away. Now, no bowl, no shapes.
There are lines of water from snow piles
following gaps in the sidewalk,
and salt crystals with nothing more to bite,
and people with street brooms cleaning the grass.
Who thinks of it as happening?
Too many of us are in the grave. We never see them.
We see this, and a gull on the open pond,
resting from dumps further in,
a neat gull, thinking nothing of it, a solution.

Alzheimer's
(for Juan)

He is praying
to canaries in a cage
on a table.

He pats leaves,
large ones, large ears
on potted plants.

He spoke to me,
he said he had considered
all things,
all things are air.

He dries his hands
on the window curtain,
removes his clothes,
bends to the canaries.

He is going now.
Or tomorrow.

Place

Roman Omen

The closed eyelid of a new moon
brushed by a string of birds
over a hill and a cupola seen
from a parapet as the sun sets red
on a city of sacred smoke.

Don't look, the city says,
I'll turn you into a pig
and let you starve in a poke.
Har, har, it says,
I wouldn't touch you,
you make me itchy.
O, this is the pits, it says,
my eyes burn from smog
and my ears are sprung.
What are you looking at? it says.
My blouse is open?
You can see a crack?
I'll show you a crack!
You take a melon
and you hit it on a post,
you eat the halves like a dog
right up to your nose!
Never speak straight, it says.
And watch the way of cats.
They only scream when loved.
You got it? Now scram!

Breakfast/Rome

The lip of my cup
is cracked, germ valley,
but the tea is drawn with steam
nothing lives in,
black tea and stays hot long,
a harsh drink
to go with peasant bread and jam
and break up time
like the pigeons on the sill
outside the clouded glass
humping or hogging crumbs
someone put there.
He has a perfect color sense,
he says, can tell painters apart,
he says, whom I lump together,
he says. So people come to him,
he says, to tell red from red,
to authenticate the artwork,
or they should, he says.
While I have a sense of voice,
I says, when it cracks and for what,
alone with itself too long.

The Messiah/Rome

There is a forum of broken temples
where cats sun themselves
on column stumps.
Next to it a park where couples smooch.
Next to it a church
where beggars work the patio.
I can take you up a street
to a fountain spitting from a wall,
or down a street to huge feet
from a colossus long gone.
Or you can stop me and I will tell you,
I want none of this
animal, vegetable, mineral silence.
Something has always been missing.
Someone has refused to stay.

Sistine Chapel: An Editorial

Clean Michelangelo's ceiling
and see what he did with incoming light,
what people did with smoke,
then what we had to see for so long,
the clear through the obscure.
There is a Sibyl's face, Eve's is like it,
and those of the naked young men,
and those fleeing the Flood,
desperate figures hauling each other up.
The forces against them are too great.
But they do not grovel.
They want to see, they want to be seen.
This is the young Michelangelo.
Clean the old man's Judgment wall
and see the saints cored of themselves,
like apples, and ready to grovel.
They want to see but not be seen.
There is one master of death.
There is one life to give and take.
Now choose between Sibyl and Saint.
The first is apricot-cheeked and alone,
looking whoever comes in the eye.
The second, baby pink, in a cluster,
and rising, like massed baloons.

The Apse at Monreale

Whoever did the Christ
was insomniac.
Each bit of stone is an open eye.
Not a dream. Not fatigue.
Not a stare.
There is pure watching
for who comes,
who goes.
The curve never closes,
never flattens.
A vigil.
The Christ is speechless.
Whoever did this
knows what is absolute,
and what is not.
The chin is balding.
The hair has a lick at the part,
escaping the comb.
The eyes are slightly right
of those who come
and go.
There are shadows.
Christ is everything and
nothing.

Whoever did this
knew a day and a night
without sleep
over someone coming
or going, uncertain which,
knew nowhere else
to be.

Roman Warning

There will be rain,
sirocco,
the roofwalk will be gritty
with Sahara sand.
People will go foolish
and know it.
Then a north wind will come,
heads will clear,
but the grit stay underfoot.
It will mix with pollen.
Then rain,
off the central mountains,
will scrub us clean.
But we go foolish in sirocco.
We think of killing,
others first, ourselves last,
off the roofwalk, with a pot
by its lily stalk,
to hit some no-tailed swift,
shut its cricket mouth!

Relation

Earth Psalm

It is hard to be equal.
I am safe weaker.
Equal, and I tell You things,
and I feel my effects.
Your silence is every form
of everything that ever was.
I know I am in love.
It doesn't matter with what.
Everything is there for speech
until our tongue is cut out
and our hands cut off.
Then there is a bird in a tree
in winter chattering
to keep its blood warm,
until our ears are stopped.
Or it bathes in dust,
until our eyes are out,
and the dust is a smell
finally clean of both of us.
But it goes strange —
random-like, in a desert,
a dust devil.

Air Psalm

Nothing but You,
and me, emtpy, waiting,
like living air.
Or nothing but me,
and confetti in people's hair,
on their noses,
and on the sidewalk later
for the wind to clear.
Tell me which.
I have other things I can be,
a gusher, a feeling gusher
with blood in my cheeks,
the taste of sex on my tongue,
and my eyes on everyone,
everything.
I am testing You.
I am switching roles.
Nothing but You,
and I am a mask with mouth
up or down, and sockets
and clean.
Or nothing but me,
and scenes
You will not forget.

Fire Psalm

You showed me the lake of fire,
but hid it under a scalloped black fog
like a cooling lava, but not gross
and literal, eating up stone walls,
just an image lake inside my head
and fog fresh from its shampoo.
But I felt the punishment pending.
It is like the presence of purity –
only the impure notice it.
You were asking me permission.
But I saw all my carnal things
and the way they lure me to live
a life of my own, not the life
of a drum and stick from the same log.
If you will not burn them with me,
I will go into that lake of fire.
If it is not You, then it is me
and suicide, and those I love
will watch cremation, and their lives
holed where I was, an acrid smell
from the burn. But if it is You,
You cannot kill, nor can You covet,
a thousand things You cannot do.

Water Psalm

If I have to open one more time
to horror or beauty, I will break.
I don't know how break next.
But please, not like the empty eyes
of the woman who sat with us
and answered questions on her poetry.
She had already killed herself.
There must be a neutral state,
like a bridge mirrored in a river
and the current rippling it enough
so no one wants a photograph.
Every time with You it's a demand
to fill those empty eyes with faces
she alone can keep alive,
or clear the bridge abutments
of a tangle of branches and debris
so they become like the tongues of cats
that lick you for affection's sake.
If You take me any further,
I will be as damned as You.
Emptiness is huge and staring.
It is the bridge without water,
the woman who tells You go.

Cain's Psalm

You left me alive,
did not burn me like a witch.
The witch is soon burned.
I think about her.
And You who sustain the fire.
I see my sin,
and You who sustained the rock.
I am now to be a flame
under someone else's control,
then brought against a skin I love
and held until there is nothing
but a gray silence,
then I am to say something!
You think I can't hear you?
Your infinite strangle?
I have nowhere to turn from it.
And You knew I would not.
My strangle is finite,
but it is Your only company.
And why you keep me.

Stations of the Cross

Drawings by Aileen Callahan

Station I

Station I – For Victim's Voices

You lose.
You are not left human.
Someone sees to it.
One order.
Soldiers work the plunger.
You suck pain,
not death, not its escape.
We hear of you later.
You are legendary.
We speak about your torture.
We know something too.
Not just what the numbers are.
We sicken easily.
We know your name and place.
Your time is up.
Ours is not.
You hear the order given.
You are left nothing.
You know it absolutely.
We do not.
We watch you for a reason.
You do not curse.
You are what we want.
Soldiers offer nothing.
You are what they leave.

Jesus is condemned to death

Station II

Station II – For Refugees' Voices

You leave a trail
as a drought or earthquake
we sort through,
animal bones, human ones,
goat, donkey, male, female,
small bird, child.
You must have walked this way,
must have bled some
on massive flags,
must have slipped on dung
on a market street,
there are seashells and fish skeletons,
or in a dump
must have been incinerated,
the carbon is featureless,
it just holds footprints
some flow of lava filled
or hot ash,
or must have stuck in melted tar
and choked standing up,
but walked here
on a road under this we are on
through a gate that's gone
with a huge crowd
you knew.

Jesus takes up his cross

Station III

Station III – For Artists' Voices

Wood, stone, flesh,
they can kiss or kill you.
They kill you here.
This is not holy wood.
This is not the rock called god,
nor flesh of anyone's flesh.
This is your collapse.
Mine can never touch it.
This is where you can't stop,
can't leave a body print,
can't get at the bowels of mercy.
It's your own you get at.
I don't say this to be savage.
I've seen your thighs in stone,
your flesh carved into wood,
seen crowds loving both,
flesh forever, blond or vegetal,
holding our mouths to a kiss.
I cannot stomach you here
because you savage me.
I want it not to be,
but beauty is your torture,
that stone shreds your knees,
that wood breaks your neck,
that body gets no mercy.

Jesus falls the first time

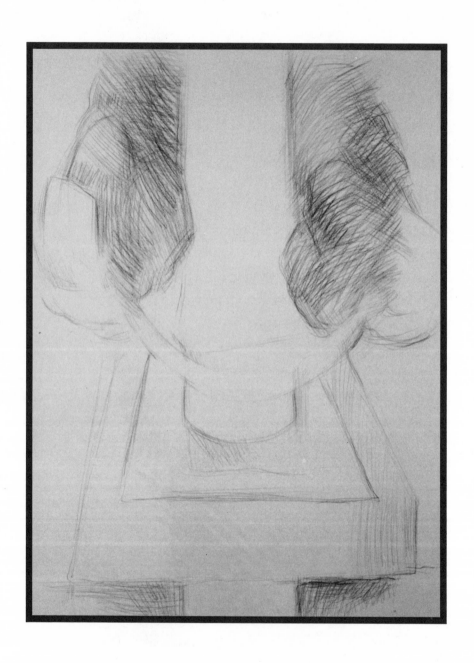

Station IV

Station IV – For Witnesses' Voices

You can't stop it.
You can't block it out.
You know who it is.
You can strangle shouting no.
You can kill yourself with frenzy.
You can die right there.
You can't stop it.
You can't touch anyone.
You know them all.
You know how far they go.
He is not finished yet.
He can take some more.
He can still breathe and see.
He has his bones intact.
He still responds to orders.
He can tell who gives them.
He knows this road.
He knows where it goes.
He knows who you are.
He dies when he sees you.
You are now the bitter sea.
You are now the bitter wind.
You know what it is.
You are now ferocious mercy.
You are tenderness inflamed.

Jesus meets his mother

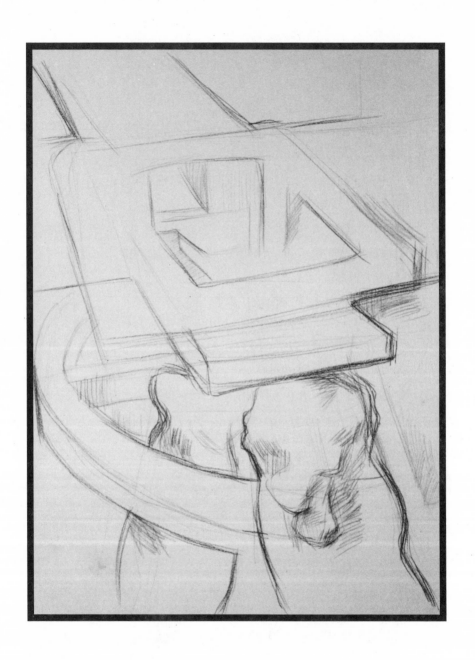

Station V

Station V – For a Man's Voice

Someone had to bend,
make bending look good,
say it was coercion,
or would cost a useless life
and didn't help at all.
It prolonged the agony.
It helped the executioners.
The contradiction is a laugh.
It would tear your heart out.
You help the executioners.
Anyone would have to.
The mercy of it is revolting.
No one knows you don't belong.
No one knows you feel differently.
No one knows you are ruined.
You come from nowhere now.
There are no consoling trees.
There is no water that tastes.
Bread is a dirty wind to breathe.
Voices execute, they never sing.
Voices call for someone's blood.
Someone says he saw you.
Someone else says thank you.
Someone rubs your shoulders.
Someone gives you food on a plate.
Someone takes your name away.

Simon helps Jesus carry his cross

Station VI

Station VI – For a Woman's Voice

Your hand can go right through.
No one can stop it.
Not the one you want to touch.
Not the ones you don't.
You have time to do something.
They have hideous distractions.
You can reach the victim's face.
You can make a mask of it.
You can know you stole it.
They will never get it back.
They will never mock it.
They will never wipe it out.
Something not torture can get through.
Something without brutality.
A hand as bared as a woman,
as bared as a man for sleep,
as a face into fruit trees,
as an arm into swarming bees.
You can ruin this game.
You can tell who you are.
No one must go by untold.
Your hand can go right through.
They will never wipe it off.
Not the one you want to touch.
Not the ones you don't.

Veronica wipes the face of Jesus

Station VII

Station VII – For Disciples' Voices

When you go down again,
we hope to die,
but there is more of you left
to strip from us.
There is our love of you.
There is our memory,
our feeling of your smooth skin,
our taste of figs from you,
our hearing of the swallows
in among the pillars,
the coat of dust from our walks,
poppies we had to sit with,
maroon and black against green
right up to the ancient walls,
a spatter of such beauty
it was blood out for a laugh.
We picked them for each other,
but they always stopped us,
made us wordlessly in love
so we left them grow in peace.
When you go down again,
it picks us clean.
We hope to die before you
like swallows, in among pillars,
who break their necks.

Jesus falls the second time

Station VIII

Station VIII – For Women's Voices

There is no way through us.
We are also the quarry.
Life is hacked from us too.
We cannot absorb you.
You must take us in
even as you have no way.
That is what we do
but do not understand.
They tie your legs together.
They buy and sell you.
They beat you blue-black
to break your soul to a mule's.
Your blood defiles them.
Your nakedness is filth.
You are ourselves.
You are our children.
They ruin your lovely skin.
They crush your eyes.
They foul your hair with spit.
They show your sex for shame.
We hide nothing from you.
There is no way through us.
We know the grave already.
We can only wash you,
Wrap you in sweet smells.

Jesus and the women of Jerusalem

Station IX

Station IX – For Survivors' Voices

Stop this,
he must be dead,
stone of a god,
stone of an executioner,
stop this up and down mob
sarcophagus,
god around us walls,
around us mountain safety,
god within us steps,
in us cisterns,
or pits for human scum,
stop this
up and down screaming
curse and grief,
eat him down under
some slab
and spare this stinking
wringing out
of flesh and blood
so bone is all that's left
to break,
god of our kilns,
our ovens,
he is baked too hard
for anyone!

Jesus falls the third time

Station X

Station X – For Victors' Voices

I saw a pit
of naked dead.
I felt a hatred
for the killers
blacken me.
I know hatred
is an evil
because of you.
I see again
your nakedness
before death.
I know you have
no hatred for
your killers,
nor any shame
to be exposed
to human torture
for a love you said
you brought.
They can strip you
naked forever.
They will find
you deeper
than their hands
can reach.

Jesus is stripped of his garments

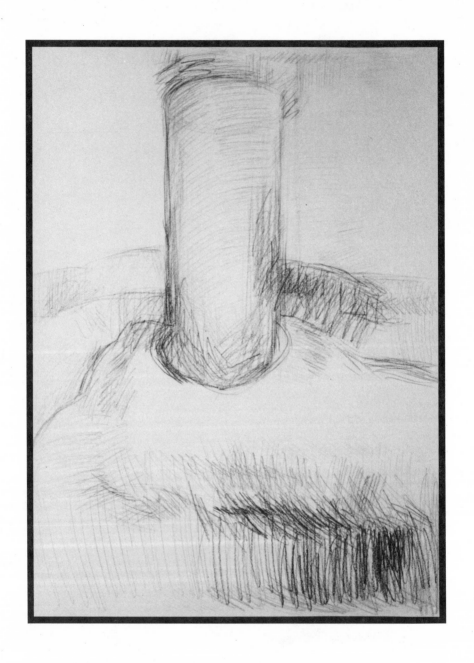

Station XI

Station XI – For Addicts' Voices

We do it
with a needle
not a spike,
yes we do,
up and down
arms and legs
so we float you
like a crow.
we did it
with a hammer
and a spike,
right on you.
we put it
to your body
as we do
with a needle
every day,
hold it right
so it won't slip
and shoot
into the blood
so quick it
takes your life
before we float it
as we do.

Jesus is nailed to the cross

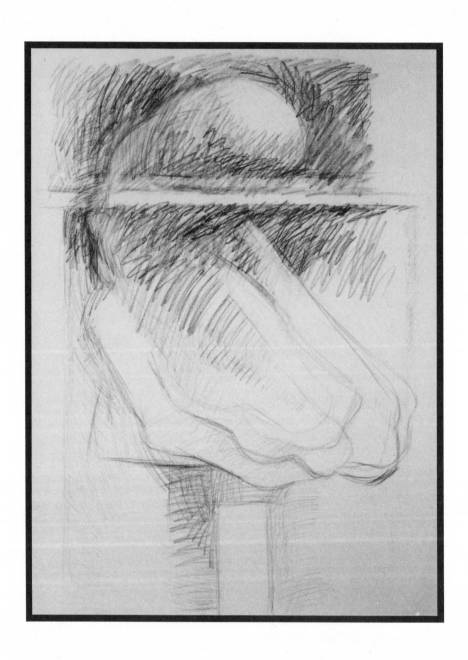

Station XII

Station XII – For Apostles' Voices

They mounted him
ferociously
to frighten us to death
because we knew him
as they did not.
He loved too much for them,
too much for us.
But it was a gift
we had no fear to take –
nor they to hate,
right in that place,
hideous place,
his breath not yet gone,
his blood not out,
his legs not fractured –
even if we wanted
never to have seen him
brutalized,
though we despaired
because we lost him.
Love can grow so cold,
we could forget
we knew
what he loved
they could not kill.

Jesus dies on the the cross

Station XIII

Station XIII – For Women's Voices

You need pure water
and a soft cloth
to clean the crusted blood
and leave his skin white.
The blue wounds
can be packed with dried,
ground orange rinds
or with powdered spice.
You need bags of balsam
to put between his legs
and under his arms
because when the stench comes,
it will beat everything
you can do to keep him
fragrant and believable.
You need for yourself
nothing but this ritual
which will do no good
and is a love like his,
fragrant and perishable.
When the orange trees blossom
next spring, you will know
what he did fills
the harsh air with beauty
everyone breathes.

                            Jesus is taken down from the cross

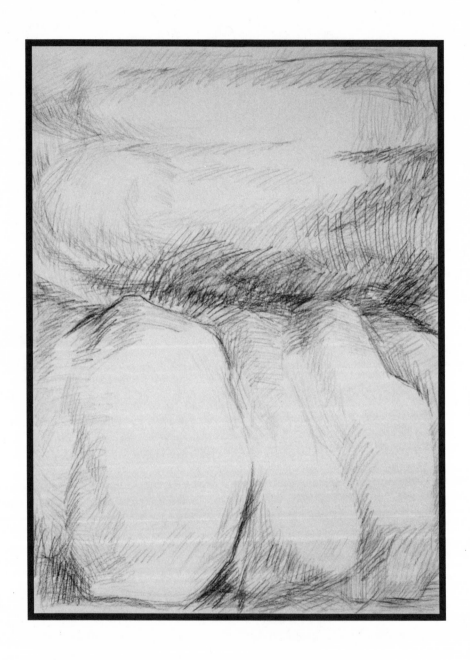

Station XIV

Station XIV – For Men's Voices

Everything else
has eaten him alive.
We wrapped him in a tomb
in a hurry
to beat the sun off
and keep him from birds
who wanted his eyes.
There was no one around
but everyone knows
where carrion is.
Now it is air and stone
that eat him
while we breathe it,
build with it.
Everything turned against him.
He is against himself now.
we can wait some years
and if we live
we can put him in a jar
like god with seas
and deeps
and think we have retrieved
our loss, but no,
his putrefaction
is too much for us.

Jesus is laid in the tomb